After the Noise Ends

After the Noise Ends

Matthew Petchinsky

1

After the Noise Ends: How Humans Reset When the World Finally Goes Quiet

By: Matthew Petchinsky

Disclaimer

This book, *After the Noise Ends: How Humans Reset When the World Finally Goes Quiet*, is intended solely for **educational, informational, and reflective purposes**. It is designed to encourage personal insight, self-observation, and thoughtful reflection on human behavior, emotional regulation, and adaptation during periods of quiet, transition, or reduced external stimulation. It is **not** a substitute for professional guidance of any kind.

Nothing within this book should be interpreted as **medical advice**, **mental health treatment**, **psychological diagnosis**, **financial guidance**, **legal instruction**, or **crisis intervention**. The author is not acting as a physician, therapist, psychologist, psychiatrist, financial advisor, or legal professional, and no professional-client relationship is created by reading this material.

The concepts, frameworks, reflections, and examples presented are **general in nature** and may not be suitable for every individual or situation. Human experiences vary widely based on biology, environment, culture, trauma history, socioeconomic conditions, and personal circumstances. Readers are encouraged to consult qualified professionals for concerns related to physical health, mental health, trauma, neurological conditions, finances, or legal matters.

Any practices, exercises, or reflective prompts included in this book are **voluntary** and should be approached with personal discretion. If at any point a reader experiences distress, discomfort, or emotional overwhelm, they should pause engagement and seek appropriate professional or community support.

The author makes **no guarantees** regarding outcomes, transformations, or results. Personal change, stability, and growth depend on individual choices, contexts, and external factors beyond the scope of this book. The reader assumes full responsibility for how the information is interpreted and applied.

By reading this book, the reader acknowledges that they are engaging with the material **by choice**, accepts full responsibility for their actions, and agrees that the author and publisher are not liable for any perceived or actual consequences arising from the use or misuse of the content.

This book respects diverse cultures, belief systems, and lived experiences and does not intend to replace personal values, professional care, or community-based support. It is offered as a reflective companion—not an authority—during moments when the noise recedes and space for awareness emerges.

Introduction

Why January Isn't About Goals—It's About Recovery

January has been miscast.

Across cultures, industries, and generations, it has been framed as a month of *pressure*: new goals, new habits, new bodies, new productivity, new identities. Calendars flip, clocks reset, and suddenly the human nervous system is expected to behave like a machine—ready to accelerate on command after months of stimulation, obligation, spending, performance, and emotional labor.

But that expectation ignores a fundamental truth:

January is not a launchpad. It is a recovery room.

By the time the calendar turns, most people are not energized—they are **overloaded**. The final weeks of the year compress family dynamics, financial strain, social expectations, disrupted sleep, sensory excess, and unresolved emotions into a single stretch of time. Even joyful moments arrive layered with noise. By January, the body is tired, the mind is cluttered, and the emotional system is quietly asking for distance, quiet, and recalibration.

This book exists because that request is usually ignored.

Instead of being allowed to rest, people are told to *optimize*. Instead of being permitted to stabilize, they are pushed to reinvent. Instead of being given space to process what just happened, they are urged to plan what comes next. The result is a familiar pattern: burnout disguised as motivation, anxiety mislabeled as ambition, and exhaustion mistaken for laziness when the drive inevitably collapses.

After the Noise Ends offers a different framework—one that treats January not as a performance cycle, but as a **biological and emotional reset window**.

Across the world, January naturally carries a quieter rhythm. Social demand slows. External expectations loosen. The environment itself—shorter days, colder air, reduced movement—signals inwardness rather than expansion. This is not a flaw in the season. It is a cue. Humans are wired to recover in cycles, and January is one of the few culturally shared moments where recovery is possible—if it is allowed.

This book does not ask you to set goals, build systems, or redesign your life.

It asks you to **stabilize first**.

You will not find rigid routines or productivity blueprints here. Instead, you will encounter a global, pressure-free approach to emotional recovery—one that acknowledges holiday overload, expectation fatigue, financial stress, social depletion, and the quiet grief that often follows prolonged chaos. The focus is not on becoming more, but on **returning to baseline**.

Because nothing meaningful grows from a dysregulated foundation.

When the noise finally ends—when obligations recede, celebrations conclude, and the world exhales—something important happens. The internal signal returns. Sensations reappear. Fatigue makes itself known. So does clarity, but only if space is given for it to surface.

January is that space.

This book is a companion for that interval between overstimulation and forward motion. It is written for people across cultures, climates, and circumstances—anyone who feels the weight of "too much" and suspects that the answer is not effort, but rest with intention.

Recovery is not failure.
Stillness is not stagnation.
And January is not late—it is right on time.

Before goals.
Before resolutions.
Before rebuilding.

First, the system must quiet.

This book begins there.

Chapter 1: The Crash Nobody Prepares You For

The Drop After the Applause

The end of the holidays rarely arrives with drama. It slips in quietly, after the last obligation is met, after the final message is sent, after the noise fades without ceremony. What follows is not relief, but a sudden internal drop—an emotional gravity that surprises people who thought they were "fine."

During high-demand periods, the human system runs on borrowed fuel. Adrenaline, urgency, social momentum, and expectation carry people forward long after their reserves are depleted. When those external drivers disappear, the body finally stops compensating. The crash is not weakness; it is delayed honesty.

This moment often feels confusing because nothing is technically "wrong." There is no emergency, no visible crisis. Yet motivation collapses, emotions feel heavy, and even simple tasks feel distant. The mind searches for a reason, assuming something must be broken.

In reality, what breaks is the illusion of sustained performance. The system is no longer being propped up by stimulation. What remains is the true state underneath months of effort, adaptation, and emotional labor.

Because modern culture does not name this drop, people internalize it. They assume the crash means failure, laziness, or loss of direction—when it is actually the most predictable outcome of prolonged intensity ending all at once.

Why the Body Always Collects Its Debt

The nervous system keeps perfect records. Every late night, every forced smile, every overstimulating environment, every suppressed emotion is logged, even when consciously ignored. During busy seasons, that ledger stays hidden behind urgency.

January is often when the bill arrives. Sleep shifts. Appetite changes. Sensory tolerance drops. Emotional reactions feel disproportionate. These are not malfunctions—they are the system attempting to rebalance after extended overextension.

People often try to override these signals with discipline or productivity tools, believing they can outwork recovery. This approach deepens the crash. The body does not negotiate with willpower; it responds to conditions.

When rest is delayed too long, recovery becomes non-optional. The crash intensifies not because the person is weak, but because the system has reached its threshold for compensation.

Understanding this reframes the experience. The crash is not an interruption of progress—it is the body enforcing sustainability where culture failed to allow it.

Emotional Lag and the Quiet Flood

Emotions often arrive late. During high-pressure periods, feelings are postponed in service of getting through the day. Joy, grief, resentment, relief, and exhaustion are all deferred until safety returns.

January provides that safety. With fewer demands, the emotional backlog surfaces. People may feel sadness without a clear story, irritability without a clear target, or emptiness where momentum once lived.

This emotional lag is unsettling because it lacks narrative. There is no obvious cause, only sensation. The mind tries to label it as depression, failure, or loss of purpose.

But what is emerging is unprocessed experience finally given room. Emotions are not appearing because something went wrong—they are appearing because suppression is no longer required.

When allowed, this emotional release stabilizes rather than destabilizes. When resisted, it turns inward, manifesting as self-criticism and shame.

The Myth of Immediate Renewal

January is marketed as a reset button: new goals, new habits, new identity. This myth assumes humans reset like software—instantly and cleanly. Biology tells a different story.

Recovery precedes renewal. Before energy can rise, it must return to baseline. Before clarity appears, noise must drain. Skipping recovery does not accelerate progress; it fractures it.

Many people experience the crash more intensely because they try to leapfrog it. They stack goals on top of exhaustion, expecting motivation to appear through force.

Instead, the system resists. Fatigue deepens. Focus blurs. Confidence erodes. The crash is prolonged because it is being denied.

Renewal that bypasses recovery is unstable. What survives long-term is what is rebuilt after rest, not what is demanded before it.

When Stillness Feels Like Threat

For people conditioned to constant output, stillness feels dangerous. Silence removes distraction. Without motion, internal states become visible.

January's quiet can trigger discomfort precisely because it reveals what was hidden: fatigue, dissatisfaction, unmet needs, and unresolved grief. The instinct is to fill the space quickly.

But this avoidance teaches the nervous system that rest is unsafe. Over time, stillness becomes associated with anxiety rather than restoration.

Learning to tolerate quiet is a skill, not a personality trait. It requires permission to exist without performing, producing, or proving.

The crash is often the first invitation to relearn that skill. It is uncomfortable because it is unfamiliar—not because it is harmful.

The Crash as a Signal, Not a Sentence

The most damaging interpretation of the January crash is that it means something has gone wrong with the person. This belief turns a temporary state into an identity.

When seen clearly, the crash is informational. It reveals where limits were crossed, where support was missing, and where recovery was postponed too long.

Responded to properly, it shortens. Resisted, it spreads. The difference is not effort, but listening.

The crash is not asking for solutions—it is asking for conditions. Less noise. Less demand. More gentleness. More time.

When those conditions are met, energy returns on its own. Not explosively, but steadily—without force.

Framework: The Recovery Before Renewal Model

This framework reframes January as a three-stage process rather than a single reset moment.

Stage One: Decompression – External demands drop, and the system slows. Symptoms include fatigue, emotional surfacing, and reduced motivation. The task here is permission, not productivity.

Stage Two: Stabilization – Sleep, appetite, and emotional regulation begin to normalize when pressure is reduced. The focus is consistency, not improvement.

Stage Three: Organic Reorientation – Only after stabilization does clarity return. Goals emerge naturally, aligned with actual capacity rather than expectation.

Skipping Stage One creates resistance. Skipping Stage Two creates relapse. Sustainable change begins only after recovery is complete.

Reflections

1. The crash is delayed honesty from the nervous system, not sudden failure.
2. Emotional heaviness often signals safety returning, not danger increasing.
3. Motivation does not disappear—it goes offline during recovery.
4. Rest that feels uncomfortable is often the rest that is most needed.
5. January reveals capacity; it does not define potential.

Quiet Recalibration

For one week, remove all language of goals, improvement, or productivity from your internal dialogue. Replace it with one question only: *What reduces strain right now?* Act on the smallest possible answer each day.

Journal Prompts

1. What did I push through in the last three months that I never processed?
2. Where do I feel the crash most clearly—in my body, emotions, or focus?
3. What signals did I ignore because I was "getting through it"?
4. What does my system seem to be asking for right now?
5. Where am I judging myself for a natural recovery response?
6. What would rest look like if I trusted it was allowed?
7. What am I afraid will happen if I slow down fully?
8. When have I mistaken exhaustion for lack of purpose?
9. What has the quiet revealed that noise kept hidden?
10. What would stabilize my days before improving them?

Closing Reflection

The crash nobody prepares you for is not a breakdown—it is a boundary finally enforced. January does not expose weakness; it exposes truth. When the noise ends, what remains is not emptiness, but information. If you listen without judgment, the crash becomes guidance. Recovery is not the opposite of progress—it is the foundation that makes progress real.

Chapter 2: Emotional Hangovers Are Real

What Lingers After the Moment Passes

Emotional experiences do not end when events conclude. The body and nervous system continue processing long after the calendar moves on. This lingering state is what many people mistake for weakness, confusion, or loss of momentum in January.

During high-intensity periods—holidays, family gatherings, financial strain, social expectations—emotions are often managed rather than felt. People stay regulated through effort, masking, or obligation. When the environment finally quiets, the emotional system completes what it could not finish earlier.

This completion feels heavy because it arrives without distraction. Joy fades, tension releases, disappointment surfaces, and relief mixes with grief. None of this is dramatic enough to be labeled trauma, yet it is significant enough to affect mood, energy, and clarity.

Because culture only validates emotions during obvious crises, these subtler aftereffects go unnamed. People assume they should be "over it" because nothing bad is happening anymore. That assumption creates shame on top of exhaustion.

An emotional hangover is simply the nervous system integrating what it endured. It is not a sign that something is wrong—it is a sign that something finally has room to resolve.

Suppressed Feelings Always Resurface

Emotions do not disappear when postponed. They wait. During demanding seasons, suppression is often adaptive—it allows people to function, show up, and meet expectations. But suppression is not erasure.

When external pressure drops, the emotional system reopens the files it closed temporarily. Old irritations resurface. Fatigue deepens. Sensitivity increases. People may feel unusually reactive or fragile without understanding why.

This resurfacing is often misread as regression. In reality, it is delayed processing. The system is doing exactly what it was designed to do when safety returns.

Attempting to suppress emotions again—through distraction, overworking, or forced positivity—extends the hangover. Integration requires acknowledgment, not avoidance.

When emotions are allowed to move through without judgment, their intensity decreases naturally. What lingers longest is not the feeling itself, but resistance to it.

Why Joy Can Also Exhaust You

Not all emotional hangovers come from stress or pain. Joy, celebration, connection, and anticipation also tax the nervous system. Excitement requires energy. Social engagement requires regulation. Happiness is not neutral—it is activating.

During holidays, people often swing between emotional highs and forced cheer. Even positive experiences require performance, timing, and responsiveness. The body does not distinguish between "good" and "bad" stimulation—it responds to volume.

After prolonged joy or celebration, the system seeks equilibrium. This can feel like sadness, emptiness, or flatness. People assume something is wrong because happiness has faded.

But what is happening is recalibration. Emotional neutrality is returning. The absence of excitement can feel like loss only when intensity has been normalized.

Understanding this prevents unnecessary self-diagnosis. Emotional quiet is not depression—it is recovery from stimulation.

The Cost of Holding It Together

Many people pride themselves on being stable during chaos. They are the ones who manage logistics, mediate conflict, and stay composed. This role carries an invisible cost.

Holding it together requires continuous self-regulation. Emotions are monitored, reactions restrained, needs postponed. The body remains alert even when outwardly calm.

When the pressure ends, that sustained effort releases. The result can feel like collapse—tears without clear cause, irritability without clear target, or profound tiredness.

This release is often mistaken for weakness because it appears after the danger has passed. In truth, it is the delayed consequence of strength.

Recognizing this reframes emotional hangovers as evidence of endurance, not fragility. The system is decompressing from the work it performed silently.

Why January Amplifies Emotional Aftereffects

January removes structure. Schedules loosen. Social demands decrease. External validation quiets. This absence magnifies internal states that were previously drowned out.

Without constant input, emotions feel louder. Thoughts echo. Sensations become more noticeable. People assume January is causing these feelings, when it is merely revealing them.

Seasonal factors—light, temperature, rhythm—also support inward processing. The environment signals rest, not expansion. When expectations conflict with this signal, discomfort intensifies.

Trying to force momentum during this period increases emotional friction. The system resists acceleration because it is still integrating.

January is not emotionally harder—it is emotionally clearer. What surfaces now would have surfaced later, often in more disruptive ways, if ignored.

Naming the Hangover Ends the Confusion

One of the most stabilizing acts is naming what is happening. When people understand that emotional hangovers are real, predictable, and temporary, panic decreases.

Naming removes personalization. The experience stops being about failure and starts being about physiology and timing.

With understanding comes patience. With patience comes regulation. The emotional system settles faster when it is not being judged or rushed.

Emotional hangovers do not require fixing. They require space, gentleness, and reduced demand.

Once integrated, clarity returns without force. Energy follows naturally. The system knows how to reset when it is allowed to finish what it started.

Framework: The Emotional Integration Cycle

This framework explains how emotions move through the system after intensity.

Activation – Emotional demand increases during events, relationships, or prolonged stress. Regulation is prioritized over processing.

Containment – Feelings are held, postponed, or minimized to maintain function.

Release – When safety and quiet return, emotions surface—often suddenly.

Integration – Acknowledged emotions settle, reducing intensity and restoring balance.

Interrupting the release phase prolongs dysregulation. Integration completes the cycle.

Reflections

1. Emotional exhaustion can follow joy as easily as stress.
2. Feelings delayed are not feelings denied—they are feelings waiting.
3. Emotional flatness is often neutrality returning, not meaning disappearing.
4. Sensitivity increases when safety increases.
5. Naming an emotional hangover reduces its power.

Quiet Recalibration

For several days, treat emotional fluctuations as weather rather than messages. Notice them without interpretation. Let them pass without assigning meaning or urgency.

Journal Prompts

1. What emotions did I postpone during the last high-demand period?
2. Where do I feel emotional residue in my body right now?
3. What feelings am I judging as "wrong" simply because they arrived late?
4. How do I usually respond when emotions surface unexpectedly?
5. What happens when I allow feelings without explaining them?
6. Where have I confused emotional quiet with emptiness?
7. What did I enjoy that may have also exhausted me?
8. What does my system do when it finally feels safe?
9. How would I treat myself if I trusted this phase was temporary?
10. What emotions might be completing their cycle right now?

Closing Reflection

Emotional hangovers are not a flaw in the human system—they are proof that it works. Feelings do not obey calendars or expectations. They resolve when space allows them to. January does not create emotional weight; it reveals what was carried quietly. When you stop fighting the aftereffects, they pass. What remains is not heaviness, but clarity earned through integration.

Chapter 3: Rest Without Guilt

How Guilt Attached Itself to Rest

Rest was not always controversial. In earlier rhythms of life, pauses followed effort naturally. Seasons changed, work slowed, and recovery was assumed. Guilt entered rest when productivity became moralized.

Modern systems reward output, visibility, and endurance. Over time, rest stopped being neutral and became suspect. If you were resting, you were assumed to be avoiding something, wasting time, or falling behind.

This conditioning runs deep. Even when exhausted, many people feel an internal pressure to justify rest. They wait until they are sick, emotionally depleted, or completely depleted before allowing themselves to stop.

Guilt emerges not because rest is wrong, but because rest threatens an identity built around usefulness. Stillness interrupts the narrative that worth must be earned continuously.

Understanding this origin matters. Guilt is not an internal truth—it is a learned response to external systems that benefit when people do not pause.

The Nervous System Does Not Respond to Permission Slips

Many people try to rest conditionally. They promise themselves a break after one more task, one more improvement, one more accomplishment. The nervous system does not recognize these bargains.

Rest that arrives after collapse is not restorative—it is reparative. True recovery requires rest *before* damage accumulates, not after it becomes unavoidable.

When rest is delayed, the body remains in low-grade alert even while "relaxing." Muscles stay tense. Thoughts continue racing. Guilt keeps the system half-engaged.

This is why people often say rest doesn't work for them. It is not rest that fails—it is rest layered with self-judgment and unfinished pressure.

Rest without guilt signals safety. Safety is the condition that allows the nervous system to downshift fully.

Why Doing Nothing Feels Like Something Is Wrong

Stillness exposes internal noise. Without tasks to manage attention, thoughts surface. Sensations become noticeable. Emotions lose their background cover.

For people accustomed to constant engagement, this exposure feels unsettling. The instinct is to reintroduce stimulation—scrolling, planning, fixing, optimizing.

The discomfort is misinterpreted as evidence that rest is dangerous or unproductive. In truth, it is simply unfamiliar. The system is adjusting to reduced input.

Doing nothing feels wrong only because something has always been demanded. When nothing is required, the system must relearn how to exist without bracing.

This relearning phase is temporary. With repetition, stillness becomes neutral, then restorative, then stabilizing.

Rest Is Not the Absence of Effort—It Is the Absence of Threat

Many people equate rest with inactivity. In reality, rest is the absence of perceived threat. You can be physically still and mentally vigilant, or physically active and deeply rested.

Guilt creates threat. Judgment creates threat. The sense that rest must be earned creates threat. Under threat, the nervous system does not recover.

Rest without guilt removes the internal watchdog. There is no timeline, no performance metric, no comparison running in the background.

This kind of rest feels different. Breathing deepens. Thoughts slow. The body releases tension it did not know it was holding.

Rest becomes effective not because more time is added, but because pressure is removed.

Reframing Rest as Maintenance, Not Reward

When rest is treated as a reward, it becomes scarce. Rewards are conditional. They arrive only after acceptable performance.

Maintenance, by contrast, is non-negotiable. Systems that are maintained do not wait until failure to receive care.

Viewing rest as maintenance shifts its timing. Instead of resting after exhaustion, rest becomes part of preventing it.

This reframing dissolves guilt. You do not feel guilty for charging a device before it dies. You do not apologize for refueling before empty.

Humans are no different. Maintenance rest preserves capacity. Reward-based rest repairs damage.

Letting Rest Be Enough

One of the hardest skills is allowing rest to be complete without adding improvement. No reflection requirement. No lesson extracted. No productivity disguised as recovery.

Rest does not need to lead anywhere to be valid. Its purpose is not to prepare you for the next push—it is to restore equilibrium.

When rest is allowed to be enough, energy returns quietly. Motivation reappears without force. Clarity surfaces without planning.

The moment rest stops being instrumentalized, it becomes effective. The system resets because it is no longer being monitored.

Rest without guilt is not indulgence. It is alignment with how human systems actually recover.

Framework: The Guilt-Free Rest Continuum

This framework distinguishes between rest that looks similar but functions differently.

Conditional Rest – Allowed only after tasks are completed; nervous system remains alert.

Negotiated Rest – Taken with time limits or internal bargaining; partial recovery occurs.

Permissioned Rest – Rest taken without justification; regulation improves.

Integrated Rest – Rest woven into daily life as maintenance; stability becomes baseline.

The quality of rest increases as guilt decreases.

Reflections

1. Guilt around rest is learned, not instinctual.
2. The nervous system recovers when threat is removed, not when time is added.
3. Stillness feels uncomfortable before it feels safe.
4. Rest works best when it is not earned.
5. Maintenance prevents collapse more effectively than repair.

Quiet Recalibration

Choose one period each day—no matter how brief—where rest is taken without explanation or purpose. No improvement, no justification. Simply allow the system to downshift.

Journal Prompts

1. What messages did I learn about rest growing up?
2. When do I feel most guilty for slowing down?
3. How do I usually try to earn rest?
4. What sensations arise when I stop without a plan?
5. Where do I confuse rest with avoidance?
6. What would maintenance-based rest look like for me?
7. How does my body signal that it needs recovery?
8. What happens when I rest without monitoring the outcome?
9. What part of my identity resists rest the most?
10. How would my days change if rest were non-negotiable?

Closing Reflection

Rest without guilt is not a luxury—it is a correction. It restores balance where pressure accumulated quietly. When rest is allowed to be complete, the system recalibrates without effort. You do not need to justify stillness to deserve it. When guilt is removed, rest does what it was always meant to do: return you to yourself.

Chapter 4: Clearing Mental Debris

What Accumulates When You Keep Going

Mental debris is not created by dramatic thoughts. It forms quietly through accumulation—unfinished conversations, postponed decisions, background worries, unresolved questions, and constant low-level input.

During high-demand periods, the mind prioritizes speed over resolution. It keeps items open to maintain momentum. Each open loop seems small, but together they create cognitive weight.

This weight is often mistaken for anxiety or lack of focus. People try to solve it by thinking harder, organizing more, or consuming new information, which adds to the pile.

Mental debris is not a thinking problem. It is a saturation problem. The mind is carrying more than it was designed to hold at once.

January exposes this accumulation because external demands pause. Without urgency, the clutter becomes visible—and uncomfortable.

Why Quiet Makes the Mind Feel Louder

When noise drops, internal activity becomes more noticeable. Thoughts that were previously masked by schedules, messages, and movement suddenly echo.

This can feel like mental chaos increasing, when in reality it is simply no longer being drowned out. The volume has not risen—the background has lowered.

Many people respond by reintroducing stimulation: scrolling, planning, multitasking. This temporarily quiets the mind but prevents clearing.

The mind does not need more input—it needs space to discharge what is already there. Silence is the condition that allows sorting to begin.

What feels like overload in quiet is often the first stage of unloading.

Open Loops Drain More Energy Than Hard Work

An unfinished task consumes more mental energy than a completed one, even if the task itself is small. The mind keeps checking it subconsciously.

During overloaded seasons, open loops multiply: "I'll deal with that later," "I should follow up," "I need to think about that." Each one occupies background attention.

By January, the system is tired not from effort, but from carrying unresolved fragments. This is why rest alone does not always restore clarity.

Clearing mental debris does not mean solving everything. It means closing loops consciously—deciding, deferring intentionally, or releasing altogether.

Resolution frees more energy than accomplishment. Closure reduces strain more effectively than progress.

Information Saturation and Cognitive Residue

Modern life floods the mind with information that does not require immediate action but still demands processing. News, opinions, alerts, advice, and comparisons linger as residue.

The mind treats this input as relevant until proven otherwise. Even ignored information leaves traces—questions, concerns, background vigilance.

Over time, this saturation blunts clarity. Decision-making slows. Creativity dulls. Mental fatigue sets in without obvious cause.

Clearing debris includes reducing intake, not just organizing thoughts. The mind cannot empty while new material continues to pour in.

Mental clarity returns not when the mind works harder, but when it is given less to carry.

Letting Thoughts Finish Their Sentences

Many thoughts remain incomplete because they were interrupted. The mind does not forget them—it suspends them.

January provides a rare opportunity to let thoughts finish. This does not require analysis. It requires allowing the mind to move at its natural pace.

When given time, thoughts resolve themselves. Some dissolve. Others clarify. A few require action. Most simply needed acknowledgment.

Interrupting this process with forced positivity or constant distraction prolongs mental clutter.

Letting thoughts finish is an act of trust in the mind's self-organizing capacity.

Clearing Is Subtractive, Not Additive

People often try to clear their minds by adding tools—planners, systems, apps, frameworks. These can help, but only after subtraction occurs.

True clearing removes excess: fewer commitments, fewer inputs, fewer internal negotiations. It simplifies before it structures.

This subtraction can feel like loss at first. Identity often attaches to mental busyness. Letting go creates space that feels unfamiliar.

But in that space, attention sharpens. Memory improves. Decision-making lightens. The mind regains elasticity.

Clearing mental debris is not about becoming empty—it is about becoming available.

Framework: The Mental Clearing Sequence

This framework outlines how mental debris naturally clears when supported.

Recognition – Notice saturation without labeling it as failure.

Containment – Write, list, or name what is occupying mental space.

Resolution – Decide, defer intentionally, or release each item.

Reduction – Decrease new input to prevent reaccumulation.

Restoration – Allow quiet for integration without forcing clarity.

Skipping recognition leads to frustration. Skipping reduction leads to recurrence.

Reflections

1. Mental fatigue often comes from unresolved fragments, not complexity.
2. Quiet reveals clutter—it does not create it.
3. Closure restores energy more effectively than productivity.
4. The mind clears when input slows.
5. Subtraction creates more clarity than optimization.

Quiet Recalibration

Choose one small mental category—messages, decisions, worries—and address only that category for a short period. Close what can be closed. Release what cannot. Stop when clarity improves, not when the list is empty.

Journal Prompts

1. What thoughts keep repeating without resolution?
2. Where am I carrying mental weight unnecessarily?
3. What information am I consuming that I do not need right now?
4. Which open loops drain the most energy?
5. What decisions am I avoiding out of habit, not difficulty?
6. How does my mind feel when nothing is demanded of it?
7. What mental noise disappears when input decreases?
8. What would I subtract before adding any new systems?
9. Where do I confuse mental busyness with importance?
10. What clarity has already appeared when I slowed down?

Closing Reflection

Clearing mental debris is not an act of control—it is an act of relief. When the mind is allowed to unload what it has been holding quietly, clarity returns without force. January offers the conditions for this clearing not because it demands reflection, but because it removes pressure. When you stop asking the mind to carry everything at once, it remembers how to move freely again.

Chapter 5: Choosing Fewer Things—On Purpose

The Hidden Weight of Too Much

Most overload is not caused by one large demand, but by many small ones accumulated without intention. Each commitment, expectation, option, and responsibility seems manageable on its own. Together, they create constant background strain.

People often believe stress comes from difficult things. In reality, it often comes from *too many* things. Even neutral or mildly positive obligations still require attention, energy, and regulation.

The mind and nervous system were not designed to track endless inputs simultaneously. When capacity is exceeded, clarity does not fail loudly—it thins. Focus fragments. Motivation scatters. Decision-making becomes heavy.

This thinning is frequently misread as a personal flaw. People assume they need better discipline or stronger willpower, when the actual issue is load, not ability.

Choosing fewer things is not about deprivation. It is about restoring proportion between capacity and demand.

Optionality Is Not the Same as Freedom

Modern life offers unprecedented choice. Options multiply in work, relationships, information, and identity. This abundance is often framed as freedom.

But optionality without limits creates constant evaluation. The mind stays alert, scanning for better choices, missed opportunities, or alternative paths.

This scanning drains energy even when no decision is made. The system never fully rests because something else is always possible.

True freedom is not infinite choice—it is reduced obligation. When fewer things are active, attention can settle instead of hover.

Choosing fewer things on purpose closes loops. It tells the nervous system that nothing else is required right now.

Why Subtraction Feels Like Loss at First

Letting go often triggers discomfort. Commitments carry identity, validation, and momentum. Removing them can feel like shrinking, even when relief follows.

This initial discomfort is the nervous system recalibrating. It has learned to equate busyness with safety, relevance, or worth.

When something is released, the system searches for replacement stimulation. The urge to fill the space appears quickly.

This urge does not mean the subtraction was wrong. It means the system is adjusting to quiet capacity instead of stretched capacity.

If the space is left open long enough, stability replaces urgency. The loss feeling fades, replaced by ease.

Fewer Things Create Deeper Presence

Attention is not infinite. When spread thin, nothing receives full presence—not work, not rest, not relationships.

Choosing fewer things concentrates attention. What remains gains depth instead of being skimmed.

This depth changes experience. Simple activities feel more complete. Decisions feel less rushed. Rest feels more effective.

Presence is not something you generate through effort. It appears naturally when the field of demand narrows.

By reducing quantity, quality improves without additional work.

Deliberate Limits Protect Energy

Limits are often framed as restrictions imposed from outside. In reality, the most stabilizing limits are chosen internally.

Deliberate limits reduce negotiation. When boundaries are clear, the mind stops debating, justifying, and revisiting decisions.

This conservation of energy is subtle but powerful. Fewer internal negotiations mean more available attention for what matters.

Limits also protect recovery. When everything is allowed, rest is constantly interrupted by possibility.

Choosing fewer things creates a container where energy can replenish instead of leak.

Choosing Is an Ongoing Practice, Not a One-Time Decision

Choosing fewer things is not a dramatic purge. It is a continuous practice of noticing when accumulation has returned.

Life adds pressure gradually. Without regular reassessment, load builds again without awareness.

This practice requires honesty about capacity. Capacity changes with seasons, health, and circumstances. What fit before may not fit now.

Revisiting choices is not inconsistency—it is responsiveness. Stability comes from adjusting before overload returns.

Choosing fewer things on purpose keeps life aligned with reality rather than expectation.

Framework: The Intentional Reduction Loop

This framework supports sustainable simplification.

Notice – Identify where energy feels thin or strained.

Name – Clarify what is contributing to the load.

Choose – Decide what stays, what pauses, what ends.
Protect – Maintain limits without constant renegotiation.

Review – Reassess regularly as capacity changes.

Reduction is not failure—it is maintenance.

Reflections

1. Overwhelm often comes from volume, not difficulty.
2. Fewer active commitments increase clarity automatically.
3. Discomfort after letting go is temporary recalibration.
4. Limits reduce internal negotiation and conserve energy.
5. Choosing less allows what remains to deepen.

Quiet Recalibration

Select one area of life—tasks, relationships, information—and intentionally reduce by one element. Do not replace it. Notice how attention and energy respond over the next few days.

Journal Prompts

1. Where do I feel stretched thin right now?
2. What obligations feel heavy simply because there are too many?
3. What am I holding onto out of habit rather than choice?
4. How does my body respond when demands decrease?
5. Where do I equate busyness with value?
6. What would improve if I chose fewer things in this season?
7. What limits would reduce internal debate?
8. What am I afraid will happen if I let something go?
9. Where has subtraction helped me before?
10. What feels easier when my focus narrows?

Closing Reflection

Choosing fewer things on purpose is not retreat—it is alignment. It brings life back into proportion with capacity. When demands are reduced, presence returns without effort. Clarity emerges without force. January offers the space to notice what has accumulated and the permission to choose differently. What remains after reduction is not less life—it is a life you can actually inhabit.

Appendix A: The January Reset Map

The January Reset Map is not a plan for improvement.
It is a **navigation tool for recovery**.

This map exists to help you move through January without forcing clarity, motivation, or momentum before your system is ready. It recognizes January as a **transitional zone**—a period between overload and renewal—where the primary task is stabilization, not reinvention.

Use this map as a reference, not a checklist. You are not meant to complete it. You are meant to **orient yourself within it**.

The Purpose of the January Reset Map

January often feels disorienting because external structure drops faster than internal recovery completes. This map restores orientation by answering three quiet questions:

- *Where am I right now?*
- *What phase am I actually in?*
- *What is appropriate at this stage—without pressure?*

The map does not push you forward. It keeps you from pushing yourself too soon.

The Five Zones of the January Reset

Zone 1: Decompression

Primary State: Fatigue, emotional flatness, mental fog

What's Happening:

Your nervous system is standing down from sustained alert. Adrenaline drops. Emotional backlog begins to surface. Motivation often disappears temporarily.

What Helps:

- Reduced expectations
- Extra sleep or stillness
- Fewer decisions
- Permission to feel "off" without interpretation

What Harms:

- Goal-setting
- Self-criticism
- Productivity pressure
- Overplanning

Orientation Reminder:

Nothing is wrong. This is the system powering down safely.

Zone 2: Emotional Integration

Primary State: Sensitivity, mood fluctuations, delayed emotions

What's Happening:

Emotions postponed during busy periods now complete their cycle. This can include sadness after joy, irritation after endurance, or emptiness after stimulation.

What Helps:

- Naming feelings without fixing
- Low-stakes journaling
- Quiet routines
- Gentle boundaries

What Harms:

- Forced positivity
- Emotional suppression
- Overanalyzing meaning

Orientation Reminder:

Emotions surfacing now are finishing old work—not creating new problems.

Zone 3: Mental Clearing

Primary State: Awareness of clutter, looping thoughts, mental heaviness

What's Happening:

Open loops, unresolved decisions, and information residue become noticeable once external noise drops.

What Helps:

- Writing things down
- Closing or consciously releasing loops
- Reducing information intake
- Simplicity

What Harms:

- Adding new systems
- Overconsumption of content
- Trying to "optimize" clarity

Orientation Reminder:

Clarity returns through subtraction, not effort.

Zone 4: Capacity Recalibration

Primary State: Desire for less, clearer limits, quieter preferences

What's Happening:

Your system begins signaling what is sustainable now—not what was expected before. Energy becomes selective.

What Helps:

- Choosing fewer commitments
- Saying no without explanation
- Slower pacing
- Respecting current limits

What Harms:

- Comparing to past capacity
- Overcommitting out of guilt
- Ignoring fatigue signals

Orientation Reminder:

Reduced capacity is not regression—it is information.

Zone 5: Organic Reorientation

Primary State: Gentle clarity, curiosity, quiet motivation

What's Happening:

Without being forced, direction begins to return. Ideas feel lighter. Interest replaces urgency.

What Helps:

- Listening rather than planning
- Small, low-pressure actions
- Letting direction emerge

What Harms:

- Forcing timelines
- Overengineering goals
- Premature acceleration

Orientation Reminder:

Direction that arrives slowly lasts longer.

How to Use the Map (Without Turning It Into Pressure)

- You may move **back and forth** between zones.
- You may stay in one zone longer than expected.
- You may never consciously reach Zone 5 in January—and that is still a successful reset.

The map is not linear. It is **responsive**.
Ask yourself periodically:

- *Which zone feels most accurate right now?*
- *What is appropriate here—not impressive?*

Then stop there.

The January Reset Rules

1. **Stabilization comes before clarity.**
2. **Clarity comes before direction.**
3. **Direction comes before goals.**
4. **Goals come last—or not at all.**

January does not require ambition to be successful. It requires honesty about capacity.

Gentle Check-In Questions (Use Sparingly)

- What is my system asking for less of right now?
- What feels unnecessarily heavy?
- What would make today easier, not better?
- Where am I rushing past recovery?
- What can remain unresolved without harm?

Closing Reflection

The January Reset Map exists because humans are not machines that restart on command. We are systems that **transition**, **integrate**, and **re-orient** in cycles.

January is not a test of discipline.
It is a window of truth.

When you use this map, you stop asking *"What should I be doing?"* and start asking *"What phase am I actually in?"*

That single shift prevents burnout before it begins.

You do not need to move faster.
You need to move **in the right direction for this moment**.

This map keeps you there.

Message from the Author:

I hope you enjoyed this book, I love astrology and knew there was not a book such as this out on the shelf. I love metaphysical items as well. Please check out my other books:

-Life of Government Benefits

-My life of Hell

-My life with Hydrocephalus

-Red Sky

-World Domination:Woman's rule

-World Domination:Woman's Rule 2: The War

-Life and Banishment of Apophis: book 1

-The Kidney Friendly Diet

-The Ultimate Hemp Cookbook

-Creating a Dispensary(legally)

-Cleanliness throughout life: the importance of showering from childhood to adulthood.

-Strong Roots: The Risks of Overcoddling children

-Hemp Horoscopes: Cosmic Insights and Earthly Healing

- Celestial Hemp Navigating the Zodiac: Through the Green Cosmos

-Astrological Hemp: Aligning The Stars with Earth's Ancient Herb

-The Astrological Guide to Hemp: Stars, Signs, and Sacred Leaves

-Green Growth: Innovative Marketing Strategies for your Hemp Products and Dispensary

-Cosmic Cannabis

-Astrological Munchies

-Henry The Hemp

-Zodiacal Roots: The Astrological Soul Of Hemp

- **Green Constellations: Intersection of Hemp and Zodiac**

-Hemp in The Houses: An astrological Adventure Through The Cannabis Galaxy

-Galactic Ganja Guide

Heavenly Hemp
Zodiac Leaves
Doctor Who Astrology
Cannastrology
Stellar Satvias and Cosmic Indicas
Celestial Cannabis: A Zodiac Journey
AstroHerbology: The Sky and The Soil: Volume 1
AstroHerbology:Celestial Cannabis:Volume 2
Cosmic Cannabis Cultivation
The Starry Guide to Herbal Harmony: Volume 1
The Starry Guide to Herbal Harmony: Cannabis Universe: Volume 2
Yugioh Astrology: Astrological Guide to Deck, Duels and more
Nightmare Mansion: Echoes of The Abyss
Nightmare Mansion 2: Legacy of Shadows
Nightmare Mansion 3: Shadows of the Forgotten
Nightmare Mansion 4: Echoes of the Damned
The Life and Banishment of Apophis: Book 2
Nightmare Mansion: Halls of Despair
Healing with Herb: Cannabis and Hydrocephalus
Planetary Pot: Aligning with Astrological Herbs: Volume 1
Fast Track to Freedom: 30 Days to Financial Independence Using AI, Assets, and Agile Hustles
Cosmic Hemp Pathways
How to Become Financially Free in 30 Days: 10,000 Paths to Prosperity
Zodiacal Herbage: Astrological Insights: Volume 1
Nightmare Mansion: Whispers in the Walls
The Daleks Invade Atlantis
Henry the hemp and Hydrocephalus

10X The Kidney Friendly Diet
Cannabis Universe: Adult coloring book

Hemp Astrology: The Healing Power of the Stars

Zodiacal Herbage: Astrological Insights: Cannabis Universe: Volume 2

Planetary Pot: Aligning with Astrological Herbs: Cannabis Universes: Volume 2

Doctor Who: Convergence Protocol – The Replicator War

Nightmare Mansion: Curse of the Blood Moon

The Celestial Stoner: A Guide to the Zodiac

Cosmic Pleasures: Sex Toy Astrology for Every Sign

Hydrocephalus Astrology: Navigating the Stars and Healing Waters

Lapis and the Mischievous Chocolate Bar

Celestial Positions: Sexual Astrology for Every Sign

Apophis's Shadow Work Journal: **:** A Journey of Self-Discovery and Healing

Kinky Cosmos: Sexual Kink Astrology for Every Sign

Digital Cosmos: The Astrological Digimon Compendium

Stellar Seeds: The Cosmic Guide to Growing with Astrology

Apophis's Daily Gratitude Journal

Cat Astrology: Feline Mysteries of the Cosmos

The Cosmic Kama Sutra: An Astrological Guide to Sexual Positions

Unleash Your Potential: A Guided Journal Powered by AI Insights

Whispers of the Enchanted Grove

Cosmic Pleasures: An Astrological Guide to Sexual Kinks

369, 12 Manifestation Journal

Whisper of the nocturne journal(blank journal for writing or drawing)

The Boogey Book

Locked In Reflection: A Chastity Journey Through Locktober

Generating Wealth Quickly:How to Generate $100,000 in 24 Hours

Star Magic: Harness the Power of the Universe

The Flatulence Chronicles: A Fart Journal for Self-Discovery

The Doctor and The Death Moth

Seize the Day: A Personal Seizure Tracking Journal

The Ultimate Boogeyman Safari: A Journey into the Boogie World and Beyond

Whispers of Samhain: 1,000 Spells of Love, Luck, and Lunar Magic: Samhain Spell Book

Apophis's guides:Witch's Spellbook Crafting Guide for Halloween

Frost & Flame: The Enchanted Yule Grimoire of 1000 Winter Spells

The Ultimate Boogey Goo Guide & Spooky Activities for Halloween Fun

Harmony of the Scales: A Libra's Spellcraft for Balance and Beauty

The Enchanted Advent: 36 Days of Christmas Wonders

Nightmare Mansion: The Labyrinth of Screams

Harvest of Enchantment: 1,000 Spells of Gratitude, Love, and Fortune for Thanksgiving

The Boogey Chronicles: A Journal of Nightly Encounters and Shadowy Secrets

The 12 Days of Financial Freedom: A Step-by-Step Christmas Countdown to Transform Your Finances

Sigil of the Eternal Spiral Blank Journal

A Christmas Feast: Timeless Recipes for Every Meal

Holiday Stress-Free Solutions: A Survival Guide to Thriving During the Festive Season

Yu-Gi-Oh! Holiday Gifting Mastery: The Ultimate Guide for Fans and Newcomers Alike

Holiday Harmony: A Hydrocephalus Survival Guide for the Festive Season

Celestial Craft: The Witch's Almanac for 2025 – A Cosmic Guide to Manifestations, Moons, and Mystical Events

Doctor Who: The Toymaker's Winter Wonderland

Tulsa King Unveiled: A Thrilling Guide to Stallone's Mafia Masterpiece

Pendulum Craft: A Complete Guide to Crafting and Using Personalized Divination Tools

Nightmare Mansion: Santa's Eternal Eve

Starlight Noel: A Cosmic Journey through Christmas Mysteries

The Dark Architect: Unlocking the Blueprint of Existence

Surviving the Embrace: The Ultimate Guide to Encounters with The Hugging Molly

The Enchanted Codex: Secrets of the Craft for Witches, Wiccans, and Pagans

Harvest of Gratitude: A Complete Thanksgiving Guide

Yuletide Essentials: A Complete Guide to an Authentic and Magical Christmas

Celestial Smokes: A Cosmic Guide to Cigars and Astrology

Living in Balance: A Comprehensive Survival Guide to Thriving with Diabetes Insipidus

Cosmic Symbiosis: The Venom Zodiac Chronicles

The Cursed Paw of Ambition

Cosmic Symbiosis: The Astrological Venom Journal

Celestial Wonders Unfold: A Stargazer's Guide to the Cosmos (2024-2029)

The Ultimate Black Friday Prepper's Guide: Mastering Shopping Strategies and Savings

Cosmic Sales: The Astrological Guide to Black Friday Shopping

Legends of the Corn Mother and Other Harvest Myths

Whispers of the Harvest: The Corn Mother's Journal

The Evergreen Spellbook

The Doctor Meets the Boogeyman

The White Witch of Rose Hall's SpellBook

The Gingerbread Golem's Shadow: A Study in Sweet Darkness

The Gingerbread Golem Codex: An Academic Exploration of Sweet Myths

The Gingerbread Golem Grimoire: Sweet Magicks and Spells for the Festive Witch

The Curse of the Gingerbread Golem

10-minute Christmas Crafts for kids

Christmas Crisis Solutions: The Ultimate Last-Minute Survival Guide

Gingerbread Golem Recipes: Holiday Treats with a Magical Twist

The Infinite Key: Unlocking Mystical Secrets of the Ages

Enchanted Yule: A Wiccan and Pagan Guide to a Magical and Memorable Season

Dinosaurs of Power: Unlocking Ancient Magick

Astro-Dinos: The Cosmic Guide to Prehistoric Wisdom

Gallifrey's Yule Logs: A Festive Doctor Who Cookbook

The Dino Grimoire: Secrets of Prehistoric Magick

The Gift They Never Knew They Needed

The Gingerbread Golem's Culinary Alchemy: Enchanting Recipes for a Sweetly Dark Feast

A Time Lord Christmas: Holiday Adventures with the Doctor

Krampusproofing Your Home: Defensive Strategies for Yule

Silent Frights: A Collection of Christmas Creepypastas to Chill Your Bones

Santa Raptor's Jolly Carnage: A Dino-Claus Christmas Tale

Prehistoric Palettes: A Dino Wicca Coloring Journey

The Christmas Wishkeeper Chronicles

The Starlight Sleigh: A Holiday Journey

Elf Secrets: The True Magic of the North Pole

Candy Cane Conjurations

Cooking with Kids: Recipes Under 20 Minutes

Doctor Who: The TARDIS Confiscation

The Anxiety First Aid Kit: Quick Tools to Calm Your Mind

Frosty Whispers: A Winter's Tale

The Infinite Key: Unlocking the Secrets to Prosperity, Resilience, and Purpose

The Grasping Void: Why You'll Regret This Purchase

Astrology for Busy Bees: Star Signs Simplified

The Instant Focus Formula: Cut Through the Noise

The Secret Language of Colors: Unlocking the Emotional Codes

Sacred Fossil Chronicles: Blank Journal

The Christmas Cottage Miracle

Feeding Frenzy: Graboid-Inspired Recipes

Manifest in Minutes: The Quick Law of Attraction Guide

The Symbiote Chronicles: Doctor Who's Venomous Journey

Think Tiny, Grow Big: The Minimalist Mindset

The Energy Key: Unlocking Limitless Motivation

New Year, New Magic: Manifesting Your Best Year Yet

Unstoppable You: Mastering Confidence in Minutes

Infinite Energy: The Secret to Never Feeling Drained

Lightning Focus: Mastering the Art of Productivity in a Distracted World

Saturnalia Manifestation Magick: A Guide to Unlocking Abundance During the Solstice

Graboids and Garland: The Ultimate Tremors-Themed Christmas Guide

12 Nights of Holiday Magic

The Power of Pause: 60-Second Mindfulness Practices

The Quick Reset: How to Reclaim Your Life After Burnout

The Shadow Eater: A Tale of Despair and Survival

The Micro-Mastery Method: Transform Your Skills in Just Minutes a Day

Reclaiming Time: How to Live More by Doing Less

Chronovore: The Eternal Nexus

The Mind Reset: Unlocking Your Inner Peace in a Chaotic World
Confidence Code: Building Unshakable Self-Belief
Baby the Vampire Terrier
Baby the Vampire Terrier's Christmas Adventure
Celestial Streams: The Content Creator's Astrology Manual
The Wealth Whisperer: Unlocking Abundance with Everyday Actions
The Energy Equation: Maximize Your Output Without Burning Out
The Happiness Algorithm: Science-Backed Steps to Joyful Living
Stress-Free Success: Achieving Goals Without Anxiety
Mindful Wealth: The New Blueprint for Financial Freedom
The Festive Flavors of New Year: A Culinary Celebration
The Master's Gambit: Keys of Eternal Power
Shadowed Secrets: Groundhog Day Mysteries
Beneath the Burrow: Lessons from the Groundhog
Spring's Whispers: The Groundhog's Prediction
The Limitless Mindset: Unlock Your Untapped Potential
The Focus Funnel: How to Cut Through Chaos and Get Results
Bold Moves: Building Courage to Live on Your Terms
The Daily Shift: Simple Practices for Lasting Transformation
The Quarter-Life Reset: Thriving in Your 20s and 30s
The Art of Shadowplay: Building Your Own Personal Myth
The Eternal Loop: Finding Purpose in Repetition
Burrowing Wisdom: Life Lessons from the Groundhog
Shadow Work: A Groundhog Day Perspective
Love in Bloom: 5-Minute Romantic Gestures
The Shadowspell Codex: Secrets of Forbidden Magick
The Burnout Cure: Finding Balance in a Busy World
The Groundhog Prophecy: Unlocking Seasonal Secrets
Nog Tales: The Spirited History of Eggnog
Six More Weeks: Embracing Seasonal Transitions
The Lumivian Chronicles: Fragments of the Fifth Dimension

Money on Your Mind: A Beginner's Guide to Wealth
The Focus Fix: Breaking Through Distraction
January's Spirit Keepers: Mystical Protectors of the Cold
Creativity Unchained: Unlocking Your Wildest Ideas in 2025
Manifestation Mastery: 365 Days to Rewrite Your Reality
The Groundhog's Mirror: Reflecting on Change
The Weeping Angels' Christmas Curse
Burrowed in Time: A Groundhog Day Journey
Heartbeats: Poems to Share with Your Valentine
Dino Wicca: The Sacred Grimoire of Prehistoric Magick
Courage of the Pride: Finding Your Inner Roar
The Lion's Leap: Bold Moves for Big Results
Healthy Hustle: Achieving Without Overworking
Practical Manifesting: Turning Dreams into Reality in 2025
Jurassic Pharaohs: Unlocking the Magick of Ancient Egypt and Dino Wicca
The Happiness Equation: Small Changes for Big Joy
The Confidence Compass: Finding Your Inner Strength
Whispers in the Hollow: Tales of the Forgotten Beasts
Echoes from the Hollow: The Return of Forgotten Beasts
The Hollow Ascendant: The Rise of the Forgotten Beasts
The Relationship Reset: Building Better Connections
Mastering the Morning: How to Win the Day Before 8 AM
The Shadow's Dance: Groundhog Day Symbolism
Cupid's Kitchen: Quick Valentine's Day Recipes
Valentine's Day on a Budget: Love Without Breaking the Bank
Astrocraft: Aligning the Stars in the World of Minecraft
Forecasting Life: Groundhog Day Reflections
Bleeding Hearts: Twisted Tales of Valentine's Terror
Herbal Smoke Revolution: The Ultimate Guide to Nature's Cigarette Alternative
Winter's Wrath: The Complete Survival Blueprint for Extreme Freezes.

The Groundhog's Shadow: A Tale of Seasons
Burrowed Insights: Wisdom from the Groundhog
Sensual Strings: The Art of Erotic Bondage
Whispered Flames: Unlocking the Power of Fire Play
Forgotten Shadows: A Guide to Cryptids Lost to Time
Six Weeks of Secrets: Groundhog Day's Hidden Messages
Shadows and Cycles: Groundhog Day Reflections
The Art of Love Letters: Crafting the Perfect Message
Romantic Getaways at Home: Turning Your Space into Paradise
Purrfect Brews: A Cat Lover's Guide to Coffee and Companionship
The Groundhog's Wisdom: Timeless Lessons for Modern Life
The Shadow Oracle: Groundhog Day as a Predictor
Emerging from the Burrow: A Journey of Renewal
The Language of Love: Learning Your Partner's Love Style
Authorpreneur: The Ultimate Blueprint for Writing, Publishing, and Thriving as an Author
Weathering the Seasons: Groundhog Day Perspectives
Valentine's Day Magic: A Guide to Romantic Rituals
The Shadow Chronicles: Stories of Groundhog Day
Love and Laughter: Fun Games for Valentine's Day
AstroRealty: Unlocking the Stars for Property Success
The Groundhog's Path: A Guide to Seasonal Balance
Groundhog Day Diaries: Reflections in the Shadow
The Groundhog's Light: Illuminating the Path Ahead
Valentine's Traditions from Around the World
AI Wealth Revolution: Unlocking the Trillionaire Mindset
Love Rekindled: Reigniting Passion in Relationships
Single and Thriving: Self-Love on Valentine's Day
Emerald Legends: Mystical Tales of Ireland
Green Alchemy: Harnessing Nature's Magic
The Hearts of Horror: A Valentine's Day Nightmare

The Leprechaun's Guide to Wealth and Wisdom
Dancing with the Sidhe: Celebrating the Otherworld
Shamrocks and Shadows: Mysteries of the Green Isle
Emerald Energy: Harnessing Luck and Growth
The Gingerbread Golem's Valentine: A Sweetheart's Guide to Love and Enchantment
The Celtic Knot: Weaving Life and Destiny
Green Fire: Elemental Magic for St. Patrick's Day
Clover Chronicles: Finding Your Inner Luck
Ireland's Mystical Creatures: A Field Guide
Gingerbread Golem's Love Almanac
Prowl and Thrive: The Lion's Guide to Success
Love Alchemy: Transforming Your Life Through Heart Energy
WORLD DOMINATION: Woman's Rule 3:The New Life
The Midnight Rose: A Guide to Lunar Love Spells
The Forbidden Letters: Writing Your Own Love Prophecy
Luck and Lore: St. Patrick's Day for Modern Mystics
The Green Path: A Pagan Celebration of Renewal
The Dark Architect's Guide to Reprogramming Reality
Prankster's Paradise: A Guide to Harmless Hijinks
Manifest Your Reality: The Law of Attraction Simplified
The TARDIS Owner's Manual: Understanding the Doctor's Ship: *A complete guide to the TARDIS, its technology, secrets, and mysteries*
Starlit Romance: Astrology Secrets for Finding True Love
The Time Lord's Atlas: A Complete Guide to the Whoniverse: ***A breakdown of the locations, planets, and dimensions explored in Doctor Who***
Sweetheart Shadows: The Dark Side of Love and Attraction
February Fire: Reigniting Passion in Every Area of Life
The Self-Love Toolkit: 5 Ways to Embrace Who You Are
February Sparks: Ignite Your Dreams in 28 Days

March to Success: A 31-Day Action Blueprint
Ancient Paths: The 13 Sacred Principles of Dino Wicca
Echoes of Tomorrow: Navigating the AI Revolution
The Wellness Blueprint: Balancing Mind, Body, and Soul
Green Horizons: Sustainable Living for a Better Tomorrow
The AI Wealth Code: How to Make Millions with Automation
AI-Powered Creativity: Writing, Art, and Music for Profit
Extinction Rites: Rebirthing Your Soul Through Prehistoric Magick
Sacred Serpents tarot
Celestial Enchantment blank journal
Star Strains
Culinary Journeys: Exploring Global Flavors at Home
The Hollowvale Curse
The Hollowvale Harvest
The Egg of Transformation: Awakening Your Inner Power
Blooming Into Power: A Wiccan Guide to Spring Awakening
The Nightmare Nexus: The Third Doctor's Perilous Haunting
Digital Detox: Reclaiming Your Life in a Connected World
Ostara's Path: Walking the Spiral of Renewal
The Sacred Hare
Financial Freedom: Building Wealth in the Modern Age
Spring's Cauldron: Stirring the Waters of Change
The Hollowvale Pact
Quantum Consciousness: The Science of Reality Shifting
The Hollowvale Hunger
The Sacred Waters Within: A Witch's Guide to Hydrocephalus Magick
The Raven's Nest: Building a Life of Unshakable Stability
AI and the Human Mind: The Future of Intelligence
The Hollowvale Reckoning
Timeless Love: Building and Maintaining Lasting Relationships

The Raven's Roar: Unlocking Unstoppable Confidence
Raven Sight: Awakening Intuition and Inner Wisdom
The Butterfly Effect: Small Changes, Big Transformations
Taming the Boogeyman: How to Conquer Your Inner Fears
The Magick of Green: Awakening Earth's Energy in You
The Entrepreneurial Mindset: Secrets to Business Success
The Hollowvale End
The Shadow Luck Ritual: Reclaiming Power from Your Dark Side
Spring Magick for Beginners: A Simple Guide to Seasonal Energy Work
Doctor Who: The Hollowvale Conundrum
The March of Miracles: Unlocking Synchronicities in Spring
Unveiling the Cosmos: A Guide to Stargazing and Space Exploration
The Ultimate Guide to Surviving an Economic Collapse
The AI Gold Rush: How to Profit from the AI Revolution
Bastet's Shadow: The Hidden Power of Feline Magick
The Bastet Codex: Unlocking the Goddess's Magickal Secrets
Purring Spells: Harnessing Bastet's Healing Frequencies
Bastet's Nine Lives: Rebirth, Transformation, and Immortality Spells
Primal Currents: Hydrocephalus Magick in the Path of Dino Wicca
The Digital Gold Rush: Mastering E-Commerce and Online Sales
Future Shock: Adapting to the Next Decade of Change
The Quantum Mindset: Think Like a Billionaire
Sacred Motherhood: Awakening the Divine Feminine Within
The Mother's Spellbook: Enchantments for Love, Protection, and Prosperity
The Witch's Guide to Parenting: Raising Empowered and Intuitive Children

The Magick of Motherhood: Reclaiming Your Power Through Rituals
The Pagan Path to Self-Love: A Goddess's Guide to Worth and Confidence
Wild Woman Magick: Unleashing Your Primal Power
The Money Magnet Blueprint: Unlocking Unlimited Wealth
Biohacking 101: Unlock Your Body's Full Potential
The Wild Father: A Pagan Guide to Strength and Wisdom
The Sacred Masculine: Unlocking Your Inner Power
The Druid's Compass
The Warrior's Mindset
The Father's Fire
Odin's Path
Ancestral Bonds
The House That Whispers
The Magician's Code
The Wild Hunt
The Green Man's Path
The Altar of Success
The Shadow and the Sword
The High Priestess's Guide to Energy Healing
The Lunar Mother
The Sacred Self-Care Grimoire
The Womb Wisdom Codex
The Wheel of the Mother
The Witch's Guide to Manifestation
The Q2 Reset
The Ultimate Guide to AI-Powered Passive Income
Escape the 9-5
AI Feline Fortunes
The Tear-Stained Grimoire
Razorblade Runes
Cemetery Sirens

The Midnight Wristwatch
The Town That Forgets
AI Horror & Creepypasta
The Hollow Frequency
The Breach Echo
The Quiet Between Worlds
The Sigil of Tharan-Khul
Summon the Vault of Y'ha'ten
The Becoming Codex
The Profit of Az'ra-nar
The Drowned Logos
Echoes of the Eldritch Will
The Deep Ledger
Necronomicon of Networth
Covenant of the Wealthwyrm
The Whisperer's Manifesto
The Rites of Azh-K'luth
The Ark of the Crawling Coin
The Tithe of Shadows
Inkheart Abyss
The Timewinds of Y'ha-nthlei
The Spiral Labyrinth of Azag-Nirrh
The Gallifreyan Heresy of the Black Pharaoh
The Psalms of Nyog-Sotha
Black Rain Alchemy
The Infinite Maw
The Entropic Blueprint
The Oracle of Sh'guul
The Book of Breach
The Drowned Saint's Testament
Dreamcraft of the Sleeper God
The Silence Market
Cthonomics: The Dark Wealth Algorithm

Invocation of the Ten-Eyed King
Wealthbound to the Wyrm Below
Become the Unnameable
Codex of the Sovereign Flame
Rituals of Relentless Becoming
The Shadow Ascends
The Eyes Beneath You
The Will That Wakes Worlds
Silence Is a Weapon
The Mirror That Screams
The Whisper Between Moments
The Mind That Devours Fear
The Myth of the Finished Self
The Architect of Your Madness
The Voice You've Buried
The Discipline of Madness
Stormborn: Awakening Your Inner Tempest
The Mind That Ate Time
Unbind Your Becoming
The Pact You Owe Yourself
The Devourer's Diet
The Acid That Carves the Path
The Tower You Must Burn
The Breath Between Worlds
Speak Like the Deep
The Labyrinth Within
The Spine of the Sea God
Rejection Is a Portal
The Crown You Refused
The Scar Is the Spell
The Lightless Flame
The Habit of Becoming Horrific
ChickenJockey Chaos

The Gatekeeper Within
You Are Not Your Name
The Compass of the Mad
The Archive of Unsent Letters
What the Mirror Can't Show You
The Knife You Needed
Worship Nothing, Become Everything
The Other Voice
The Body the World Forgot
The Vein of the Void
The Black Bone Codex
The Puzzle of the Hidden Self (Millennium Puzzle)
The Eye That Sees the Lie *(Millennium Eye)*
The Ring of Return (Millennium Ring)
The Rod of Relentless Will ***(Millennium Rod)***
The Tally of the Soul (Millennium Tauk/Necklace)
The Key to the Locked Timeline (Millennium Key)
The Scale of Sacred Decisions (Millennium Scales)
Inferno Bites: The UnOfficial Minecraft Lava Cookbook
Rot in the Attic
Prana: The Hidden Force of Your Infinite Self
The Shadow Realm Within: Transforming Darkness Into Destiny
The Borderland Collapse
Claws of Protection: Bastet's Defensive Magick
Mr. Ring-a-Ding's Madness
Yugioh Astrology: Celestial Deckcraft and Duel Destiny (2026–2027 Edition)
The Seal You Signed: Unlocking the Power You Once Feared
The Puzzle of Infinite Minds: Unlocking the Mentalism Hidden Within
The Eye That Mirrors the All: Secrets of Inner Reflection
Doctor Who: The Toymaker's Broadcast

The Rod of Eternal Flow: Commanding the Currents of Vibration
Golden Eyes of Bastet: Enhancing Psychic Vision
The Key of Dual Forces: Balance Within the Polarity
The Scales of Living Rhythm: Timing the Dance of Life
The Necklace of Hidden Cause: Weaving the Webs of Fate
The Ring of Secret Masters: Rising Through the All Within All
Daggers of the Dying Deep
Bastet's Wealth and Fortune Magick: Prosperity Rituals of the Goddess
The Tide that Speaks
The Scrolls of Petosiris: 13 Rituals from the Feathered Eye
Petosiris and the Living Plague of Osirion
Feline Fire: Bastet's Passion and Love Magick
The Star Altar of Petosiris
Bastet's Whiskers: Supernatural Sensory Magick
The Bastet Grimoire
Feeding the Shadows
The Mouthless Prayer
The Spiral Wound
Becoming the Ibis: Lessons from Petosiris's Mind
The Crimson Coven: Cola Magick for Sweet Dominion
Sacred Cat's Paw
The Soda Zodiac: A Flavor for Every Sign
Covenant of the Crawling Flame
The Ink of Ish'Zur
Frothroot: The Thirst That Ate the World
The Golden Glyphs of Prosperity
The Etherbind Codex
Echoes of the Resistance: Reclaiming the You That Survived
Harnessed Minds: Breaking Free from Mental Control
The Eyes in the Smoke

Rootwake: The Carbon Covenant
Skitter Logic: Unlearning the Fear That Built You
Doctor Who: The World That Froths
Rootwake: The Fizz That Rewrites Flesh
Rootwake: Frothfather of the World
The Holly Pact: Blood Beneath the Mistletoe
The 2nd Mass Principle: Building Unbreakable Tribes
Web of Wits: A Survival Guide to Encounters with Anasi the Spider (Aunt Nancy)
The Hexbreaking Handbook: Effective Spells to Remove Curses
Pop Alchemy: Transform Your Life One Sip at a Time
The Mason Code: Leading in Unleadable Times
Petosiris and the Fifth Chamber of Thoth
The Ether Seed Within
The Parent of Tomorrow
Petosiris's Pyramid of Perpetual Wealth
Unlearn the World
Grimoire of the Hollow Tongue
Zodiac Weeds: Finding Your Strain Through the Stars
Aquarius Rises in the Bank
The Sugar God's Smile
The Skinclock Reversal: Biohacking the Face of Time
Debtburn: How to Obliterate What You Owe Forever
The Ice Cream Oracle: What Your Cone Says About Your Future
Silence Is Sovereignty: The Power of Being Unreadable
The Wind That Whispers Through Stone
Path of the Four Directions
Doctor Who: The Maestro's Symphony of Endings
Oxygen Grail: Breathing to Undo the Clock
Zodiacal Collapse: When Stars Devour Time
Teachings from the Red Sand Silence

Doctor Who: Omega – The Broken Equation
Memory Wipe Your Past: Start Over Like a MiB
Mitochondria Prime: Ignite the Core of Youth
A Nest of Roaches
Grub from the Galaxy: MiB Recipes You'll Never Forget
Whiskers of Power: Bastet's Guide to Inner Sovereignty
The Gift Must Cost Them: Negotiation Through Unequal Exchange
The Worm Guys' Wealth Code: Hustle Like an Alien
Bug Out: The Edgar Method for Ruthless Goal Setting
Weaving Life with Spiderwoman's Pattern
Doctor Who: The Rani's Renaissance
How to Get a Job (If You're a Puppygirl)
Speak Through Others: The Art of Proxy Power
T-Rex Your Trauma: Reclaim the Power of Your Primal Self
The Black Briefcase: How MiB Stay Wealthy in Silence
The Thirst Beyond Reason: Understanding Diabetes Insipidus From the Inside Out
Backwoods Witchcraft for Billionaires: The Pagan Path from Dirt Roads to Gold Roads
The Moonshine Grimoire: Fermented Spells for Abundance
The Nameless Geometry
The Wraith's Mixtape: Spellcasting with Songs of Sorrow
The Gallifreyan Gentleman: Silent Wealth, Sonic Confidence, and the Doctor's Code of Living
Sugar Water Confidence
Dino Totems: Spirit Guides from Earth's First Gods
Pumpkin Sigils & Ritual Smoke
The Hózhó Compass
The Distortus Discipline – Order from Inner Mutation
Witchcraft for the Cold-Blooded Soul
Moonlight Over the Blessingway
Water, Interrupted: When the Body Forgets How to Hold On

Deformed but Divine: Embracing Your Asymmetry

Hexes in the Henhouse: The Farm Witch's Guide to Power

The Reversed Flame: A Grimoire of Inverted Power

Salt, Cells, and Sanity: Reclaiming Balance with Diabetes Insipidus

King of the Broken: Crowning the Flawed Self

Moonlight Scars: Emo Moon Magick and the Art of Lunar Sorrow

Noose Spells: Magick of the Hanging Rope

The Goth Cathedral: Rituals of the Broken and Beautiful

The Cretaceous Codex: Dino Spirits and Fossil Magick

The Turkey Bones Ritual

Nine Lives of Manifestation: Unlocking Bastet's Reality Codes

Chaos Muscles: Building Strength from Twisted Pain

Emo Blood Magick: The Veins of Power

The 3AM Flood: Nighttime Urination, Sleep Loss, and the DI Spiral

The Silence Between the Stars

The Lemon Method: Sour Your Way to Success

Starlit Sovereign

The Rite of Twelve Gates: Walking the Gates of the Duat.

Cornbread and Conjure: Recipes for Riches and Rootwork

The Black Rose Rituals: Emo Love Spells and Obsession Magick

The Eternal Goodbye: Death Magick and Rebirth Rituals

Sinkrot: The Drain That Remembers

The Hybrid Mindset: Thinking Beyond Evolution

Bone Dry: Navigating Dehydration Before It Breaks You

Wreathcraft: Winter Sigils and Yuletide Spells

The Rite of Twelve Mouths

S'mores of the Damned: Haunted Recipes for Halloween Night

Rethink the Drink: A Beverage Survival Guide for DI Warriors

The Shadow Chord: Guitar Magick and Sonic

Malformed Yet Majestic: Leading When You Feel Wrong Inside

The Cursed Diary: Ink-Stained Spells of the Emo Soul

Anxiety Off Switch: Emergency Reset for a Fried Nervous System

The Energy Heist: How to Take Back Your Life from Drainers

Beyond the Bathroom: Rebuilding Your Social Life With DI

Coyote's Gift for Decision Makers

Ghoul-Goo: Spooky S'mores You'll Die For

Echoes in the Mirror: Scrying and Self-Destruction Magick

Thread and Thorn: Stitching Spells from Rural Cloth

The Mogwai Mind: Building Untouchable Wealth from Small Ideas

Be Your Own Guide: Trust Your Inner Compass

Hormones in Chaos: The Endocrine Puzzle of Diabetes Insipidus

ChronoCleanse: Detox Your Biological Timeline

The Limb You Hide Is the One That Saves You

Leaves, Bones, and Whisper Spells

The Dinosaur Mindset: Prehistoric Tactics for Modern Wealth

Clawing Back Control: A Bastet Method for Boundaries and Empowerment

Samhain Codes of the Forgotten

Orange Alchemy: The Autumnal Spellbook

Monster Within, Master Without

The Sigil That Sleeps

Hearthcraft: Yule Hearth Sigils and Winter Warmth Spells

Temple of the Purring Moon: Rituals from Bastet's Lineage

When the Earth Remembers Your Footsteps

Food for Mood: Eat to Heal Depression, Not Just Survive It
Witch of the Kudzu Vine: Southern Pagan Wealth Secrets
The Invisible Diagnosis: Advocating for Yourself With DI
The Coffin's Lullaby: Sleep Magick and Nightmares as Portals
Ashes of the Will: Rituals for Erasing the Self
The Fracture Rite: Shattering the Magickal Core
Funeral Candles: The Art of Emo Flame Magick
The Black Grimoire: A Blank Ritual for Writing in Absence
Phantom Thirst: A Halloween Survival Guide for Diabetes Insipidus
The Hollow Crown: Emo Royalty and Magick of the Outcast King
Sandpainting for the Soul
Falling Into Balance: Using the Extra Hour to Recalibrate Life
100 Southern Superstitions That Still Work
The DI Child: A Parent's Guide to Raising Hydrated, Happy Kids
The Jungle of Shame: Escaping the Hidden Lab of Doubt
The Witch's Toast: S'mores Spells and Creepy Confections
The Hoodoo Pantry: Spells from the Mason Jar
The Immortal Fortune: Secret Wealth Lessons from Captain Jack Harkness
The Specter's Embrace: Magick for Channeling Ghostly Lovers
Grateful Waters: A Thanksgiving Survival Guide for Diabetes Insipidus
The Seizure Gospel
Harvestbind: Autumn Sigils and Samhain Spells
Doctor Who: The Algorithmic Awakening
Silent Nights, Steady Waters: A Christmas Survival Guide for Diabetes Insipidus
The Extra Hour Effect: How One Hour Can Transform Everything

Blade Between the Breaths
Running with the Mountain Shadows
Echoes of the Failed Experiment – Becoming a Living Legacy
Swamp Witches & River Ghosts: Real Southern Hauntings
Cornbread Prophecies: Magical Recipes from a Southern Table
Doctor Who: The Signal in the Star
Bloomcraft: Spring Sigils and Equinox Enchantments
Vanisher: How to Disappear from the Internet Without Losing Your Life
The Ultimate Christmas Cookie Cookbook
The Unbreakable Parent: How to Mentally Survive Raising Kids in a Broken World
Time Debt: How to Reclaim the Hours You Didn't Know You Lost
One Month, One Million: Unconventional Cash Creation Tactics
Doctor Who: The Cyber Conversion Protocol
Black Friday Frenzy: The Art of Finding Hidden Online Deals
The Grimoire Buried Under the Apple Tree
Digital Couponing Masterclass: Your Step-by-Step Guide to Black Friday Savings
The Fire Inside the Flint
Shadows on the Ceiling: The Emo Guide to Astral Magick
The Bone-Eaters Beneath Us
Black Friday Bundle Blueprint: Creating Irresistible Product Packages for Maximum Sales
Thirteen Nights of Unbinding
Doctor Who: Engines of Influence
Pumpkin Spice Alchemy: Recipes of Fire and Frost
When Raptor Met Rexy: Prehistoric Lessons in Wild Romance
Oblivion's Candle: Burn the Path Behind You

Campfire Curses and Chocolate: A Halloween S'mores Grimoire

The Wallet That Wasn't Mine: Breaking Free from Inherited Scarcity

The Cola Zodiac: What Your Fizz Says About Your Fate

Frostfire Fortune: Unlocking Winter's Hidden Prosperity

Signal Jamming: Detox Your Brain from Info Overload

The Dust of the Forgotten Rite

The Golden Cat Sigils: Drawing Power in Bastet's Name

Mud Magick: The Prosperity of Getting Dirty

Savory Spicefall: Beyond the Pumpkin Pie

Pumpkin Spice Apothecary Kitchen

The Pumpkin Spice Economy: Turning Trends into Billions

The Ember Veil: 13 Nights of Fire Magick

Financial Freeze: When Earning Triggers Panic

The Gingerbread Alchemist: Sweet Recipes with a Twist

Biosynth Power: Programming Yourself from Scratch

Echoes from the Talking Circle

Truffle Alchemy: Fungus of Fortune

Spores of Power: The Truffle Witch's Handbook

Doctor Who: The Tower That Speaks

The Mycelium Veil: Truffle Magick Unbound

Broke But Ashamed: Healing the Shame Wound of Debt

The Evergreen Mind: Growth Through Winter Stillness

The Black Veil Truffle Rite

The Voice Beneath Symbols

Witchlight on the Bayou: Swamp Spells for Sovereignty

I Grew Up Poor and Now I Sabotage My Success

The Lantern of Hollow Souls

Shutdown Survival: A Citizen's Guide to Thriving When Government Stops

When Abundance Feels Like a Threat: Healing the Hidden Fears of Enough

The Scarecrow Grimoire
Owls of the October Veil
Candlewax and Curses: A Halloween Spellbook
Excavating the Inner Fossil – Transforming Fossilized Thoughtforms into Tools of Power
The Yule Witch's Spellbook: Magick for the Holiday Season
Haunted Christmas: Ghost Stories for Winter Nights
The Christmas Survival Guide: Thriving Through the Chaos
The Bone Orchard Rites
Haunted Commerce: The Ghost in the Marketplace
When Money Triggers the Inner Child
Silent Night with the Silence: A Christmas Thriller
The Lightning Crown: Living and Leading Through Seizures
TARDIS Tidings: Festive Stories from the Whoniverse
Autumn Reset: Slowing Down Without Falling Behind
The Trillion Dollar Soul: Rewriting the Currency of Reality
Truffle Eclipse Magick
Micro-Manifestations: Quick Magick That Works
5-Minute Rituals for Busy Witches
The Marshmallow Massacre: Halloween Treats with a Sinister Twist
Blood and Blackberry Thorns
Magickal Mornings: Rituals for a Blessed Christmas Day
Embers of the All-Hallows Fire
The Pumpkin Market Collapse
The Hour You Gained: Transforming Time Into Power
The Chamber Must Be Sealed: Mastering the Power of Controlled Access
The Cursed Manuscript of Petosiris
The Festive Hearth: Creating Holiday Traditions
Darkness Rising: Thriving as Nights Grow Longer
Harvesting Time: Turning the Year's End Into Your New Beginning

Petosiris and the 13th Zodiac Key
Wagewound: When Paychecks Become Identity Prisons
Walls That Watch
The Silent Feast: Rituals of Power in the Longest Night
The Distortus Legacy : Becoming a Deformed King in a Perfect World
The Hollow Masks
The Gratitude Furnace: Forging Gold from Thanks
Feast of Inner Gold: Eating for Energy and Enlightenment
Haunted Commerce: The Season of Spending Spirits
Fear Bonds: How Panic Creates Profit
Black Friday E-Commerce Playbook: Sales Tactics to Skyrocket Your Holiday Revenue
Budgeting for Black Friday: A Holiday Savings Planner
Haunting the Harvest Moon
The Warrior's Water: Emergency Preparedness for People With DI
The First Sip of the Year: A New Year's Survival Guide for Diabetes Insipidus
Doctor Who: The Thirteenth Node
The Unseen Struggle: Mental Health, Anxiety, and Chronic Thirst
The Hearth's Hidden Ledger: Counting Energies as Currency
The Gift Alchemist: Turning Any Offering Into Gold
The Papyrus of the Bound Spirit
The Magick of Leftovers: Transmutation in the Fridge
Frost and Fortune: Christmas Wealthcraft for the Modern Magus
Last-Minute Gifts: Creative Ideas on a Budget
10 Secrets to Surviving Holiday Crowds
The Witch's Dow Jones
The Witches' Graveyard Shift
Pumpkin Sigils: Carving Rites for Midnight Power

The Secret Shopper's Black Friday Guide: How to Get Early Access and VIP Deals

Fever in the Foundation

The Neuralyzer Reset: Reprogram Your Morning Routine

Lightning Lessons of the White Painted Woman

The Enchanted Snowflake

The Magic Sip: Surviving Disney Parks with Diabetes Insipidus

The One Who Draws Through You

Santa's Secrets: A Magical Holiday Planner

Silent Bells, Loud Miracles: Self-Help for the Season of Stillness

The Sugar Spell Codex: Confectionary Magick of Christmas

Autumn Hexcraft: Fallen Leaves, Fallen Barriers

Sleep Like a Fortress: Build a Life Where Insomnia Can't Survive

Nowhere Was Ever Home

Christmas Under the Stars: A Celestial Holiday Guide

Rentproof: How to Never Be Evicted Again

Workless: Escape the 9-5 Without Being Broke

The Gilded Gift: A Wealth Altar for Christmas Morning

The Black Friday Grimoire

The Hollowing: Ceremonies of Spiritual Collapse

Doctor Who: The Nameless Signal

Where the Eagle Hides His Courage

The Dwarf Tyrant's Ascent: Claiming Power in a World of Giants

The Currency of the Dead: Trading with Spectral Bankers

The Icebound Witch: Survival and Magick in the Cold

The Emergency Money Mind: Constant Crisis, Zero Calm

Thirst & Roses: A Valentine's Survival Guide for Diabetes Insipidus

Springing Into Clarity: Mastering the Energy Shift of Daylight Saving

Speed of the Nanotyrant: Agile Strategies for Life's Hunt

The 90-Day Reset: A Science-Backed Guide to Reinvent Yourself Before the New Year

The Coil of Thorns

Timegates Unleashed

Dopamine Fasting 2.0: Rewiring Your Brain in a World of Overstimulation

The Nanotyrannus Mutation: Embracing Your Differentiated Form

Unwritten January: How to Use the Blank Page of the Year to Re-Author Your Life

Feast of the Forgotten Spirits: Ancestor Magick for the Holidays

The Burnout Codex: A System for Thriving Beyond Stress

I Don't Deserve to Have Money

When the King Doesn't See You: The Shadow Predator's Guide

The Reset Ritual :A Guide to Shedding Last Year's Weight—Emotional and Physical—by Spring Cleaning Your Soul

Calendar Alchemy: Learn to Bend Time and Productivity around Your Natural Rhythms

The Mirror Contract: A One-Sentence Agreement with Yourself that Unlocks Real Change

The Nile Formula: Sacred Flow for Millionaire Minds

Forward Momentum: Productivity Rituals for the Lost Hour

Harvest Gold: Wealth Magick of Pumpkin Spice Commerce

The Magick of Christmas Lights: Illuminating Holiday Rituals

Cranberry Crown: Royal Self-Worth through Ritual Meals

Petosiris and the Worms of the Feathered Throne

The Evergreen Equation: Self-Help for Sustained Growth

The Rain Will Wash Us Away: Emo Weather Magick

Snowlight Shadows: Magick Under Frozen Stars

Doctor Who: Merger of Empires

The Light Within the Feast: Magickal Wealth of Yuletide Flame

Momentum Machines: Small Habits Designed to Snowball into Unstoppable Forward Motion

Calm Spells: Magickal Solutions for Anxiety Relief

Santa's Final List: The Naughty Never Leave

The Mystic's Guide to Banishing Worry

The Silence Dividend: Turning Quiet Mornings into Compounding Growth All Year

Charmed Stillness: Rituals to Ease the Mind

Blood Spiral Ascension

The Vanishing Heart Invocation

Crystal Calm: Harnessing Stones for Anxiety

The Nano Tyrant Code: Strength in the Small Predator

The Energy Ledger: Accounting Methods for Vitality, Not Just Money

Snowglobe Mindset: Shake Up Your Thoughts, Settle Into Peace

The Weight of the Feather: Anubis's Codes for Soul Balance

Pocket Peppermint Power: Tiny Rituals for Big Holiday Energy

Shadowkeeper of the Golden Jackal: Anubis's Path to Energetic Protection

The Witch's Breath: Anxiety Relief Through Magickal Breathing

The Tiny Ember: Pocket Motivation for Cold Days

Stocking Sorcery: Mini Spells for Holiday Luck and Prosperity

Warm Hands, Steady Heart: Micro Grounding for Winter Anxiety

The Jackal's Lantern: Guide-Lights for Walking the Dark Path

Anubis's Silent Steps: Rituals for Stealth, Peace & Emotional Quiet

The Bonewake Protocol

Extinction-Proof: How to Outlive Trends, Trauma, and Time

The Fourth Doctor: The Eccentric Wanderer

The Second Doctor: Chaos and Charm in the TARDIS (Patrick Troughton, 1966–1969)

The Third Doctor: Earthbound Defender of Time (Jon Pertwee, 1970–1974)

The First Doctor: Genesis of the Time Lord (William Hartnell, 1963–1966)

The Fourth Doctor: The Eccentric Wanderer ***(Tom Baker, 1974–1981)***

The Fifth Doctor: Elegance and Empathy (Peter Davison, 1982–1984)

The Sixth Doctor: A Kaleidoscope of Conflict (Colin Baker, 1984–1986)

The Seventh Doctor: The Strategist of Shadows (Sylvester McCoy, 1987–1989)

The Eighth Doctor: A Time Lord's Renaissance (Paul McGann, 1996)

The War Doctor: A Time Lord's Burden (John Hurt, 2013)

The Ninth Doctor: The Healer of Worlds
(Christopher Eccleston, 2005)

The Tenth Doctor: The Lonely Hero (David Tennant, 2005–2010)

The Eleventh Doctor: The Madman in a Box (Matt Smith, 2010–2013)

The Twelfth Doctor: The Rebel with a Cause (Peter Capaldi, 2013–2017)

The Thirteenth Doctor: Breaking the Mold
(Jodie Whittaker, 2017–2022)

The Fourteenth Doctor: A New Beginning (David Tennant, 2022–2023)

The Fifteenth Doctor: Rewriting the Stars
(Ncuti Gatwa, 2023–2025)

Santa's Shortcut to Success: Micro Habits for a Better New Year

The Midnight Cocoa Manifesto: Comfort Rituals for Hard Nights

Why I Can't Save: Trauma Blocks to Financial Planning

Dino Brain, Mega Goals: Rewire Yourself for Savage Success.

Jurassic Profit: Unearth Your Inner Millionaire Fossil

Scales & Softness: Dating with Dino Heart

Carnotaurus Dreams.

Red Willow Thinking.

Reindeer Resilience: How to Keep Going When You're Exhausted

Candlewick Courage: Lighting Strength in Dark Seasons.

Elf-Mode Focus: Fast Attention Fixes for Busy Seasons

Futureproof Feelings: Emotional Skill-Building for Resilience No Matter What the New Year Brings

The 90-Day Rewire: Transform Your Neural Pathways Before Spring Blooms

Jolly Rich: Christmas Micro-Money Magick for Fast Prosperity.

Gingerbread Gratitude: Mini Practices for a Happier Holiday

Trauma-Spending: When Money Becomes a Drug

Goal Skeletons: Build Minimalist Frameworks for Resolutions That Last

The Snarl Strategy: Growling Back at a World That Silenced You

The Hourglass Reset: Reclaiming What the Clock Took

Yule Claw: Dino Rites of Light in the Darkness

Sacred Circles: Grounding Rituals for Anxious Souls

Clockstopper's Gut: Rebuilding the Core of Time

Winterfire Drive: Harness the Cold Season's Stillness to Ignite Deep Motivation

The 5-Minute Productivity Hack: Small Steps to Big Results

Light Ascending: A Self-Help Guide to Longer Days

Inner Economy: Trade Self-Doubt for Confidence Like a High-Value Currency

Simple Success: Decluttering Your Life for Better Results

The Resilient Mind: Thriving in Tough Times

The 2026 Playbook: Mastering the Year Ahead

The Spring Sleep Solution: Conquering Fatigue After Time Change.

The Hormonal Compass: Navigate Back to Your Youth

Golden Vision: Eating for Your Eye Color with the Power of Ghee

Lionhearted Love: Strength in Relationships

MiB Mindset: Think Like a Cosmic Agent

The Ladder of Small Wins: Climb Out of Stagnation by Stacking Micro-Victories

The Momentum Hour: Gaining More in Less Time.

The Year of You: A Self-Help Blueprint for Unapologetic Self-Ownership

The Dust That Watches You Back.

The Astral Parent

Shadow of the King: The Nanotyrannus Parable

Tiny Tidings of Triumph: Small Wins That Change Your Life

Dwarf Tyrant Rising: When You're the One They Overlook

The Bank Account Mirror: Healing How You See Yourself Through Money

Cretaceous Black

When Love Costs Too Much: Romantic Triggers and Financial Wounds

Dream-Eater's Guide to Wealth

Unzipped Reality: The Jacket That Opens Portals

The Power of No: How to Set Boundaries and Get Rich

Keeper of the Desert Veil: Anubis's Teachings on Illusion & Truth

Redacted Stargates: Stories the SGC Buried

The Clock That Dripped Time

Doctor Who: The Silent Acquisition

Hairline Manifestation: Unlocking Power at the Edge of Thought

Cash-Eater Crickets: How Insects Predict Economic Collapse

Dead Pet Whisperer: Grief Alchemy from the Other Side

The Love Algorithm Is Broken: Hack Romance Before It Hacks You

The Rite of the 8-Limbed Seal

Melt the Moon: A Fire Ritual to Reshape Emotion

Venomous Miracles: Healing Through the Poison Path

Wealth Without Water: The Post-Aquatic Rich Life

The Butterfly Betrayal: When Change Turns on You

The Quiet Upgrade: How Humans Are Secretly Rebuilding Themselves Without Asking Permission

Nobody Taught Us This: The Missing Human Manual for Money, Energy, and Self-Respect

You Were Never Broken: Why Most People Are Reacting Normally to an Unstable World

Get Some Tarot cards: https://www.makeplayingcards.com/sell/apophis-occult-shop

Get some shirts: https://www.bonfire.com/store/apophis-shirt-emporium/

Instagrams:
@apophis_enterprises,
@apophisbookemporium,
@apophisscardshop
Twitter: @apophisenterpr1
Tiktok:@apophisenterprise
Youtube: @sg1fan23477
Hive: @sg1fan23477
CheeLee: @SG1fan23477

Podcast: Apophis Chat Zone: https://open.spotify.com/show/5zXbrCLEV2xzCp8ybrfHsk?si=fb4d4fdbdce44d

Newsletter: https://apophiss-newsletter-27c897.beehiiv.com/

If you want to support me or see posts of other projects that I have come over to: **buymeacoffee.com/mpetchinskg**

I post there daily several times a day